BETWEEN US AND THE STARS

SAMANTHA LOPEZ

BETWEEN US AND THE STARS

SAMANTHA LOPEZ

SAMANTHA LOPEZ

© Samantha Lopez

copyright © 2020 by Samantha Lopez. All rights reserved. No part of this book may be used or reproduced in any manner whatsoever without any permission except in case of reprints in the context of reviews.

Samantha Lopez
@orbitingvega
lyralopez144@gmail.com

For Mom and Dad,

The brightest stars of all.

SAMANTHA LOPEZ

ACKNOWLEDGEMENTS

Poems would not exist if there were nothing to write about. If I hadn't been living this life, with these circumstances and these people, I would not be publishing this book. So if you know me, and you're reading this book, chances are you are a part of it.
Firstly, I'd like to thank my parents, who have given me a life worth living, a happy life; my family for supporting me and shaping me into the me I am today; my teachers and professors, for giving me a place to grow; my friends for growing with me.
Paola, for everything, per tutto.
And thank you, dear reader, for giving my words a chance to speak.

BETWEEN US AND THE STARS

"I am constantly trying to communicate something incommunicable, to explain something inexplicable, to tell about something I only feel in my bones and which can only be experienced in those bones."

-Franz Kafka

SAMANTHA LOPEZ

HUMANS

I am made and remade continually.

Different people draw different words from me.

-Virginia Woolf

BETWEEN US AND THE STARS

We were tragically
And hopelessly
Broken,
Crushed under the weight
Of our own
Infinities.

SAMANTHA LOPEZ

Let's meet in those picture-perfect places
And then maybe
We'll be perfect too.
Let's build our house there,
Let's plant our trees,
Let's run wild and maybe
We'll finally be free.
Let's chase our dreams to those unreal places
And then maybe
We'll realize that we
Never
Really
Left.

BETWEEN US AND THE STARS

We breathe in
The smoke
Of our burning cities.
The kingdoms that once belonged to us.
We stand on our hill
And just watch them
Burn.
There was never a more beautiful hell
Than the one we left.

SAMANTHA LOPEZ

We're all playing our own game,
With our own rules,
And we claim
We're winning.

BETWEEN US AND THE STARS

Fondled up
Behind the curtain,
The promises we left before the show.
No one remembers how to love
As pride welcomes us to take our seats.

SAMANTHA LOPEZ

I thought
I just thought that those days weren't nothing.
But I was wrong,
Nothing means anything except what we want it to mean
and I thought I had gold when actually I had dust.
But it felt like gold, I swear, pure gold.

BETWEEN US AND THE STARS

This is who you are,
What are you going to do with all this you?

SAMANTHA LOPEZ

I was scared of the dark,
Knowing enough things about it.
But I was more scared of the darkness I couldn't see,
The one on the other side of me, hidden.
A secret darkness made of demons and monsters.
A hell.

BETWEEN US AND THE STARS

Feelings are so much more than words,
But we use those to define the way we feel.
So how can it ever be even close to accurate?
How can we not be misunderstood?

SAMANTHA LOPEZ

Maybe you mattered
Maybe so did I
But it was the us that made a difference.

BETWEEN US AND THE STARS

Another promise gone to dust

SAMANTHA LOPEZ

I miss a memory that once made me smile.
When songs meant something and something meant you.
You were there
And so was I
Tangled in what would become a "remember when"
That would fade and get lost in the years
Where you're there
But I'm not.

BETWEEN US AND THE STARS

You stood there
Like the world was yours
Like there was nothing anyone could do to steal it from you.
With your crown
Like a king
You were unreachable
So far away.
Do you remember me?
I used to stand beside you.
When the sky was bluer and our smiles were brighter.
God we were an impossibility
A living miracle.

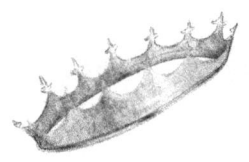

SAMANTHA LOPEZ

I wish you had smiled
The world froze to give us both enough time
The gods wanted to see which one of us would break first.
But you didn't recognize me
And I was too stuck in my head to live on the first try.

BETWEEN US AND THE STARS

Some words are sticky
And others are sticks.

SAMANTHA LOPEZ

And yet you still linger in that quiet space
between sleeps

BETWEEN US AND THE STARS

I've thought so many thoughts about you
Written so many words
Because in my head memories went on forever
Repeating
Reliving
Ad infinitum

SAMANTHA LOPEZ

I can still see you smiling at me
from the shadows of the past
God, I wish I could look away,
I wish I would stop coming back to a memory
That leaves me standing alone with ghosts.

BETWEEN US AND THE STARS

I enjoy seeing your face

SAMANTHA LOPEZ

What's the point of living if everything will eventually
disappear into nothing
What's the point if nothing will be left of us
Love poems, Impressionist paintings,
Pyramids and Greek temples.
All gone.
Forgotten.
A whole history, everything that once inspired us,
moved us, reminded of our greatness and limitations.
Forever lost.
Like footprints in the sand.

BETWEEN US AND THE STARS

I followed your eyes
Oceans uncharted

SAMANTHA LOPEZ

I miss you with every ounce of memory in my body

BETWEEN US AND THE STARS

How unsatisfying to live in a present uncontaminated
by the past.
What an easy way to live
What a fragile escape from a doomed
Universal
Condition

SAMANTHA LOPEZ

You've always been the type who could burn bridges
with just a look.

BETWEEN US AND THE STARS

It takes time and distance to really appreciate the beauty of what we no longer have.

SAMANTHA LOPEZ

We consume memories
Like the soles of our shoes,
Walking down familiar roads
Revisiting the past,
An old friend.

BETWEEN US AND THE STARS

Even the sky knew you were leaving

SAMANTHA LOPEZ

I've cried again tonight

BETWEEN US AND THE STARS

IN-BETWEEN

"To live, would be an awfully big adventure"

-Peter Pan

SAMANTHA LOPEZ

I had rebellion written on my arms.
I followed the letters that ran across my skin
To the great end that sat on the tip of my fingers.
E-N-D
And then the lines stop.

BETWEEN US AND THE STARS

I spend so much time with the stars
I forget what it means to be human.

SAMANTHA LOPEZ

I wrote down
What I felt,
But turns out
They were just
Words.

BETWEEN US AND THE STARS

I'm a skeleton under my skin,
Living a dead thing's life.

SAMANTHA LOPEZ

We're bones and skin,
Both dead and alive.
We are what we were
When time was beyond us,
What we will be
When it forgets us.

BETWEEN US AND THE STARS

The sun is shining, warming my ankles.
It's the distant call of spring.
So far, but too close it's terrifying.
The orange-brown color palette reminding me there's still time,
Still a minute left before the bell rings
And the sun will stop shining.
Spring is gone,
It's winter already.
I missed summer because I blinked.
I blink again,
The leaves are falling.

SAMANTHA LOPEZ

I sit here
Unable to fall.
The sky is so far up,
Locked away in another time
Another space.

BETWEEN US AND THE STARS

Il cielo grigio pesa sulle mie spalle,
Sono in ginocchio
Aspettando che crolli.

The gray sky weighs on my shoulders,
I'm on my knees,
Waiting for it to fall.

SAMANTHA LOPEZ

I live in between worlds
Jumping from one reality to another
No one really enough to fill the voids I create
Each time I run away,
No one satisfying my insatiable thirst of
Belonging.

BETWEEN US AND THE STARS

I need a break to catch my breath
Everything is moving too fast
Casting shadows under the moon
Days turn into nights so quickly
I feel like I'm awake
While I'm still dreaming

SAMANTHA LOPEZ

Reliving our lives backwards to really live them once.

BETWEEN US AND THE STARS

So many people
So many feet
And hands
And eyes
And moving lips.
I see them all as one
Existing together
All at once
Quantum

SAMANTHA LOPEZ

I wanted both extremes
And was cursed to live in between.

BETWEEN US AND THE STARS

So many lives I could have lived

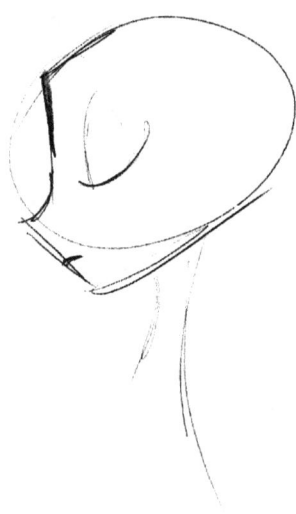

SAMANTHA LOPEZ

A small bee buzzing endlessly close to my feet
So close
So close
I step carefully on the grass
One step
Two steps
Just a few more
Bees crying. The sound deafening.
Loud and getting louder
I can't go back
The past is forbidden
And so I carry on, trying not to forget
The reason why I was crossing the world in the first place.
To die for survival.
One sting as worthy as a small sting
A life for a small remark
A one syllable word
A temporary tattoo
Is it really worth it?

My feet are the only part of me that exists
Everything else
Part of the air.

BETWEEN US AND THE STARS

We're like glass cups on the edge of a coffee table.
So unable to live
Tormented by the clingy feeling of death.

SAMANTHA LOPEZ

Homeless
Trapped in a dimension that's not really there
Forced to live in in-between
Half one
Half the other

BETWEEN US AND THE STARS

I feel like summer is coming at me like a storm
A storm full of rain and hope.

SAMANTHA LOPEZ

And I sit here
Between hope and despair
With the knowledge that something has to happen
And the scary shiver that whispers
"It's up to you"

BETWEEN US AND THE STARS

Why does this not feel real?
Why am I always stuck looking through my mind
Disconnected from the world
My feet not touching the ground
My body
Inexistent
Like a kite
In the sky

SAMANTHA LOPEZ

I've walked on rose bushes
The thorns digging into the soles of my feet
Blood as white as milk
Pure and silky white. As white as milk.
A little bee
Buzzing by my toes
All black and yellow
Wings and stripes
I step off the concrete
I'm into the clouds
Above it all
No wind or world
No bees or bushes
Roses or thorns
Just air
Rich and empty.
They carry me in all my humanness
With all my skin and bones
I am weightless,
A mass with two eyes and a nose.
You lost me
Above the horizon.

BETWEEN US AND THE STARS

I am dissolving
Losing touch with the world
Back in my head
Stuck
In my own body
Which has become a prison
Forgetting
Not living
Maybe not even dying
Or both
Maybe an in-between
Yes
Of course
An in-between.

SAMANTHA LOPEZ

Goodbyes
Hit harder
At night.
Like thunder
In the dark
Even louder
After the lightning.

BETWEEN US AND THE STARS

As hard as we may try
There's nothing we can do to stop the future
From hunting us down.

SAMANTHA LOPEZ

Sometimes,
The thought of being alive is enough
To exhaust me.

BETWEEN US AND THE STARS

Find me a place to rest
A place to let go of the past
A place to store my memories and the selves I've had to be
To be the me I am today
The me I still don't recognize.
Help me get to a place where I no longer feel the need
To hide
To run
To cry
Help me find a home.

SAMANTHA LOPEZ

I can no longer cry,
Tears make it hard to see
I need my eyes
I need to see
Being blind will only make it harder.

BETWEEN US AND THE STARS

It's all planned
And it will drive you insane.

SAMANTHA LOPEZ

STARS

"Toda la vida es sueño, y los sueños, sueños son."

-Calderón de la Barca

BETWEEN US AND THE STARS

When the lights go out
That's when it's really the
End.
And we'll wait.
We'll just stare out at the darkness that's left,
Enjoying the only slightly annoying ring of silence.
Waiting to see what comes
After.

SAMANTHA LOPEZ

Our eyes are the most important things we own.
They are
The rabbit holes to
Wonderland.

BETWEEN US AND THE STARS

We wanted to set the sky on fire,
Write our names with indelible flames,
Like the stars
Unforgettable.

SAMANTHA LOPEZ

She had a star on her left cheek,
Right below her left eye,
That shone every time she used her light.
She was brave but she wasn't fearless
She was a hero but she wasn't invincible.
Every so often
Stars die too.

BETWEEN US AND THE STARS

I'm capturing words
Like fireflies at night.
Watching them glow under their own light.
How bright
They burn
To light the way

SAMANTHA LOPEZ

I just had to look up to see the world.
Fields
The sun
The sky
A piece of infinity
And you had that in your eyes.

BETWEEN US AND THE STARS

Through your eyes
The world is lovely

SAMANTHA LOPEZ

You walked along the edges of the map
Thinking you wouldn't fall
Or maybe thinking you would
Hoping
Falling into something new
Unknown
Infinity you called it
There is no room for infinities on a map.
You were ready for what was uncharted.

BETWEEN US AND THE STARS

Let us stare at the stars and wish it was us
Burning so brightly
On the verge of infinity.

SAMANTHA LOPEZ

Under these skies we sleep on gold.
Like kings we dream.
A lost kingdom
Of broken swords.
And in the wind
We drift.
Forgotten kisses
I left on your cheek.
You are the stars,
I swear,
You are light.

BETWEEN US AND THE STARS

Right on the edge,
Before the drop,
My breath in my throat,
I
Step
Off
And watch the world fly.

SAMANTHA LOPEZ

Forgotten on a shore
My head on a chest.
A pirate's curse.
I open it
And let it kill me.

BETWEEN US AND THE STARS

I've been falling in love with the colors that lay behind you
The colors of your shadow,
The ones you cannot see.

SAMANTHA LOPEZ

I'll never get used to the way the light kisses the grass,
Falling from the tree branches.
The way it lays there
Staring up at where it came from,
As peaceful as one who knows what it means to be
Home.

BETWEEN US AND THE STARS

To fall in love with life
What a beautiful and brave jump

A free fall into infinity.

SAMANTHA LOPEZ

Friday,
Even in the rain,
You feel like summer.

BETWEEN US AND THE STARS

Phoenix

My heart is shattered
But it was already dust
There was no reason to hope
All that was left
Burnt to ashes.
I look down at my wrist
"You wish"
And hope grew wings.

SAMANTHA LOPEZ

You deserve a sunset over a field of violets.
You deserve to sit there,
Holding her hand,
Watching him run with his shadow on his heels.
You deserve so much more than a hospital bed.
White walls, all pain and grief.
For a better present,
In a near future.

BETWEEN US AND THE STARS

It will only grow darker.
So smile, sweet child,
For this world needs light.

SAMANTHA LOPEZ

The sky's above me,
That's all I need.

BETWEEN US AND THE STARS

Acknowledgements 4
Humans 6
In-between 35
Stars 64

SAMANTHA LOPEZ

www.ingramcontent.com/pod-product-compliance
Lightning Source LLC
Chambersburg PA
CBHW031456040426
42444CB00007B/1121